Parenting the Crisis Generation

A Child Psychiatrist's Top Strategies
for Intervention and Healing

Jean Young Bai, MD

The people mentioned in this book are loosely based on the author's experience, and the identities of the patients have been changed to protect their privacy.

Copyright © 2024 by Jean Young Bai, MD

Paperback ISBN 9798218546991
Ebook ISBN 9798218547004

Cover design: Cover Designs by Karen
Book Interior Design: Karen Fuller

Table of Contents

For my father, who instilled the love of reading in me; For my mother, who believed that I could write this book; For my husband and my two children, who inspire me.

INTRODUCTION

Parenting is the most difficult yet rewarding job in the world. I thought staying up all night on call at the hospital during my medical residency was the most challenging period in my life. But that was a breeze compared to pulling all-nighters comforting a gassy infant or sending the children off to their first day of school. Yet the benefits outweigh the pain, and we persevere. You know it's worthwhile because you would do anything to protect your child, even taking a bullet if it came to it.

Parenting is a balancing act. It is not only physically draining but mentally demanding as well. When someone talks about a balancing act, what images come to mind? For me, it's a circus clown with a long stick balanced on each hand and a plate spinning at the pinnacle of both sticks. If you are lucky (and old enough), you might have actually seen this act on stage. You think it's a matter of time before the plates come crashing down, but somehow, the clown manages to balance and spin the plates until the very end. Only the clown knows how many plates were broken during rehearsal.

At the time of this writing, I have been working as a child and adolescent psychiatrist at an urban community mental health center for more than fifteen years. I've treated an array of mental health challenges experienced by hundreds of diverse youths and their families over the years. Their problems were distinct in detail but similar in theme, which led me to believe that families were making the same mistakes repeatedly. By the time they came to see me, their negative behavior patterns had persisted for years, and they were often resistant to change.

I wrote this book for caring parents/ guardians/mentors like you, so I could help you learn from the mistakes of countless others in order to avoid heartaches of your own. I am also writing to help erase the stigma of mental health diagnoses and make it clear that your child is not suffering alone. Because the stigma remains, too many families are afraid to talk about their child's mental health and ask for help.

In December 2021, almost two years after the first case of COVID was diagnosed in the US, the US Surgeon General officially declared a national mental health crisis among our children and adolescents.[1] In short, many families across America are in the same boat.

---

1 "The U.S. Surgeon General's Advisory." HHS.gov, 6 December 2021.

Just how bad is the crisis? According to the US Surgeon General's report, "Youth Mental Health: The Surgeon General's Advisory," emergency departments saw a 51 percent increase in suicide attempts among adolescent girls.[2] In addition to the academic disruption and social isolation COVID brought, many young people also lost parents and their access to food, housing, and social services.

But the COVID epidemic isn't the only factor here. In truth, the youth mental health crisis had been brewing for many years prior to the pandemic. According to the US Centers for Disease Control and Prevention, one in three high school students reported persistent feelings of sadness and hopelessness in 2019. That represented a 40 percent increase from

2 Yard, Ellen. "Emergency Department Visits for Suspected Suicide Attempts Among Persons Aged 12–25 Years Before and During the COVID-19 Pandemic - United States." *Morbidity and Mortality Weekly Report*, vol. 70, no. 24, 2021, pp. 888–94.

2009.[3] Suicide rates increased by 57 percent in youths ages 10 to 24 between 2007 and 2018.[4]

Preventative care can do much to help alleviate this crisis, as is the case with any public health emergency. This book will not only provide you with preventative strategies and effective interventions but also provide you with a list of resources you can use to find help.

I have organized this book into three parts. In Part One, I will share an extended story of a boy I call Dustin. His story doesn't belong to any one patient of mine. Rather, it's an amalgamation I created from the stories of hundreds of patients. I encourage you to read the entire story, so you can make the best use

3 "Youth Risk Behavior Surveillance Data Summary & Trends Report: 2009-2019." Centers for Disease Control and Prevention.

4 Curtin, Sally. "State suicide rates among adolescents and young adults aged 10–24: United States, 2000–2018." *National Vital Statistics Reports*, vol. 69, no. 11, p. 3.

of the information that follows.

In Part Two, I will use excerpts from the story as the basis for eleven lessons so you can avoid these common mistakes. These lessons will help you parent a struggling youth much more effectively. They include guiding a child with mental health challenges such as ADHD, autism, depression, and anxiety.

In Part Three, I will introduce you to several young people in crisis. They are youths who have experienced suicidal ideation and self-harm; trauma and abuse; or bullying and eating disorders. I want to help you recognize the warning signs yourself and understand what can happen next. In each of the scenarios, I will discuss recommendations for effective action.

I hope this book becomes a treasured family resource and that you find it useful enough to recommend to friends and family when they share their heartaches.

PART ONE
DUSTIN'S JOURNEY

Dustin's first memory was fighting with a boy in daycare. The other child was a giant, maybe twice his size. The mammoth boy straddled him and pummeled his face while sweat dripped down from his enemy and mixed with Dustin's blood. A teacher tried to break up the fight, but the other boy was too strong and resisted her.

After it was over, Dustin couldn't remember how long the bashing went on or the reason for the ruckus. He did recall that his mother came to pick him up and argued with the teacher. Their heated exchange ended with his mother's tears, and she abruptly took his hand and dragged him out of the building.

It was also the first time he saw her cry.

Over the years, he saw her sob too many times. Sadness was her frequent companion. He thought his mother wept so incessantly because of his misdeeds, so he tried so hard to please her. He tried sitting in class quietly like the others, but a motor drove him from the inside that he couldn't calm. He tried raising his hand to answer his teacher, but words came out of his mouth that annoyed her, and she made him stand frequently in the corner. The other kids ridiculed and bullied him, so he fought to defend himself. Soon he was labeled as the troublemaker in his class, and nothing he did could change his title.

Even when he did have periods of good behavior, especially around Christmas when his mother promised him a video game he wanted, his mother still cried. He was baffled by her misery. He didn't have many

memories of his father since he left them
when he was an infant, but he wondered if
she was saddened by his absence.

He didn't know life with two parents,
a father he could emulate, and a mother
who smiled. His classmates had fathers
and mothers who came to the classroom
parties, and he often saw the parents laugh
and fuss over their children, but no one
ever showed up for him. His mother had to
work constantly to feed and clothe him, so
she could never make it to the parties. He
wondered what his father was like, since he
was never discussed in the household.

On occasions when he pressed his mother,
she yelled and screamed at him to never
mention the man. He pondered what his
father must have done to give her so much
pain. He thought it must be something terrible
adults did to each other. Even by third grade,

he knew too much of the world, since his mother left him with babysitters who were preoccupied with their phones. So, he roamed the Internet as freely as he wished. When his mother did come back from work, she often slept and stayed in her room.

On the Internet, he saw terrible things, especially regarding what men and women did to each other. There was so much violence that already existed and even more that people made up. He couldn't tear his eyes away from that brutality, since he realized it excited him. He scoured the Internet looking for more disturbing images and bloodshed, each time worse than the last. Was this how people normally treated each other, or how they were supposed to behave? He also saw what people did to themselves, how they hurt themselves to deal with sadness.

Even at that young age, he knew he was

sad himself. He thought about his despondent mother, his worthless father, and the poverty they lived in. He only saw endless suffering that stretched before him, and he even thought about ending his life. Would his mother miss him if he died? Or would it add to her sadness? He thought about the rope in the closet and how easy it would be to tie it around his neck and end the anguish. He took it out to touch its roughness. He went so far as to feel its tightness around his neck.

But he couldn't kill himself because of the voice of his grandmother in his head. She was the only one in his life he could remember who showed kindness and affection toward him. She cuddled him to sleep when he had nightmares. She bandaged his knees when he skinned them and kissed them to heal faster. She told him about a place a person went after death, only if he made good choices. She took him to church and taught him more about the place beyond death. He wanted to make good choices because he loved his grandmother, but he still couldn't control his impulses that were always one step ahead of him. So, when his grandmother succumbed to COVID-19, he was devastated. The doctors tried to save Grandma, but she continued fading away. He went to see her in the hospital only to see tubes coming out of her in all directions. His grandmother reached for him and told him to be brave and good, so she could see him in heaven one day. Before long, she died.

When Grandma died, all the light went with her. Dustin cried for days and didn't know when his tears would end. He didn't understand the pain in his heart and how it hurt incessantly. At some point, he got so tired of his sadness that he let anger take over. It was easier to deal with anger and hate rather than the unrelenting pain in his heart.

In school, Dustin became the bully. It felt good to channel his anger and direct it toward someone else. He usually picked the smallest kid in the class to torture. He relished the power he had over another, the power to break another's soul, because he felt so broken himself. He also became destructive when anger took over. Even a slight remark could unleash his rage. He found himself hurtling chairs across the room, ripping paper off the walls. His teachers called his mother constantly to pick him up and keep him home for several days. His mother yelled, threatened, and even begged him to stop the havoc since she had already lost several jobs. However, he couldn't calm the storm that raged inside him, no matter how hard he tried.

His teachers asked his mother to get him

some help so that he could quiet his mind. They told her that there was a name for his anguish, and once named, he could start the healing process. However, his mother ignored their pleas because she was afraid of those institutions that asked questions and judged her. She knew deep down that she was at fault for her son's anguish, and it was easier to bury her guilt and hide her shame rather than expose herself. She would rather deal with the constant barrage of complaints from the school than be forced to examine her own broken soul.

However, his mother couldn't hide any longer once the state became involved. His mother often had attacks of rage herself, and she threw a glass cup at him when he asked about his father again. The glass shattered against the wall, and a piece had cut his face. His mother immediately jumped to bandage his wound, but the damage was already done. He went to school the next day, and his teacher asked what had happened to his face. He told her about his mother and her outbursts, and he found himself crying. Once the tears started, he couldn't stop. His teacher took him to the counselor's office, and he stayed there for the rest of the day.

The counselor was a lady with warm eyes. She gave him an endless supply of tissues and waited patiently for him to stop crying. Once he was able to stop, she asked him questions about his mother and his house. He answered her as best as he could since he wanted to impress her. Here was someone who showed him kindness like his grandmother, and he craved that warmth. After he answered all her questions, she said she was going to call his mother to come and pick him up. He wasn't fazed by it since it happened often enough.

However, what came next was surprising.

***

A few days later, a man came knocking on their door. He wore a tie and carried a brown leather briefcase with him. Since they didn't have a doorbell, his knock became louder and louder. His mother usually ignored strangers, but this man was persistent. She opened a crack and asked what he wanted. The man said that he was from the state's children and youth protective services and that someone had made a complaint about child abuse, so he had to come to investigate. His mother was furious and tried to close the door, but the man jammed his briefcase through the door so she couldn't close it. He gave her his card and said that if she didn't cooperate, there would be consequences from the law. But if she cooperated, the investigation should be brief.

His mother reluctantly opened the door to let him in. He sat on their living room couch and asked many questions. He asked Dustin's mother about the cut on her son's face and how it came about. She fumbled with her words and made up a story about how he was clumsy and fell on a broken piece of glass. The man asked to speak to Dustin alone, and he told him exactly what had happened. The man looked around the house and in their fridge to make sure they had enough food and that the house looked safe enough to live in. Afterward, he told them that he would get back to them with the results of the investigation.

When he came back, he told his mother that she had to take him to a local mental health clinic. He gave her a list of numbers she could call. If she didn't, she would have to face consequences from the law. At this point, his mother didn't have a choice. She dreaded it, but she made the call to get him an appointment.

***

On the day of his appointment, Dustin followed his mother into a five-story glass building. They wandered among the maze of corridors and people speaking in hushed voices. His mother asked for directions several times and managed to lead them to a room full of people waiting, staring into their phones. In one corner, he saw a basket full of toys and a table of unused puzzles. Even the youngest child in the room had their eyes fixed on their phone, tapping and swiping with frenzy. Occasionally, someone came out of the room and called a name. Some of the

children bounced up and followed the men
and women who came out of the closed office
doors. Others dragged their feet and walked
as if they were going to their execution.
Finally, a man came out and called Dustin's
name. He sat frozen in his seat, suddenly his
heart pounding. *What secrets would I have to
reveal now?* His mother looked at him, and
he saw the same fear in her eyes. She got up,
took his hand, and pulled him out of his chair.

Once Dustin was seated in his counselor's
office, he took a good look at the man and
thought he had kind eyes like his counselor
at school. But he was older and taller than
the counselor. He wore a blue sweater, baggy
jeans, and an earring in his left ear. When he
entered the man's room, he was surprised
by the assortment of toys in all its nooks and
crannies. Several model airplanes hung on
the ceiling, and remote-controlled cars sat in

the corners of the room. A giant whiteboard dominated an entire wall. The kind man told him that he could play with the toys while he talked to his mother.

He knew his mother was nervous because she kept clenching her jaw. But the man had a way about him that made her feel at ease. He asked her questions but didn't press her if she couldn't answer. He even got her to crack a smile at his jokes. Dustin couldn't remember the last time his mother smiled. When it was Dustin's turn to talk, the man asked his mother if she could leave the room so he could talk to him alone. Dustin felt his palms sweat as he looked at his mother. She told him to answer honestly and walked out of the room.

"Come and sit on this chair," the man said. He walked to the chair next to his desk and sat.

"Do you like any of the toys you see here?" he asked.

"Umm, maybe the remote-controlled car … the red one," he answered.

"Yeah, lots of kids like that one. I saw you playing with it. You must have figured out quickly how it works," he said.

"It wasn't too hard," he said.

"So, what's a smart kid like you doing in a place like this?" the man asked with a smile on his face.

"I don't know. My mom said I had to come," Dustin said.

"Why do you think she brought you here?"

"Not sure. Maybe it had to do with the cut on my face?" Dustin wanted to impress the man. He wanted to show him that he could be as cool as his toys that filled the room.

"Oh, that. Yes, tell me more about that day …"

From that day on, his mother took him to talk to the man, Mr. Lee, once a week. During the warm and sunny days, they took the remote-controlled cars out to a small sitting area just outside the building and talked while they battled the cars against each other. Dustin told Mr. Lee about his miserable life, how he missed his father that he never knew, and how he craved love from his sad mother. He told him about his grandmother and how his heart broke after her death. But he couldn't tell him about the rope and how he tightened it around his neck. He was afraid that Mr. Lee would get upset and, even worse, tell his mother about what he did.

Mr. Lee also talked to his mother alone, and they spoke with him together. He noticed some changes in his mother. It was very subtle, but he saw it nevertheless. He saw her smile when she thought no one was looking.

She yelled at him less and walked away to go to her own room to scream like Mr. Lee told her to do. When he saw that she was sincere about improving herself, he wanted to match her resolve. But it wasn't always smooth sailing. They fell back to their old patterns often, since it was easy and familiar. They yelled and screamed at each other, and his mother still received phone calls from school. But Dustin felt a shift in himself. There were people who cared about him, including his mother, and he knew he could tell Mr. Lee about anything. Someday, Dustin would tell him about the rope in the closet when the time came. He didn't want to talk about it at the moment. Besides, he didn't really think about it anymore.

***

Dustin talked incessantly about his desire to see his father, so Mr. Lee intervened. His mother didn't like the idea at first. She got up from the chair and almost walked out of the room when Mr. Lee mentioned that it was time for Dustin to see his father. But she calmed herself down to hear what Mr. Lee had to say. Eventually, she agreed to let her son see his father during therapy. She agreed to drop Dustin off and stay in her car so she wouldn't have any encounter with his father. Mr. Lee would call her when the father left so she could pick Dustin up to go home.

The day came when Dustin would meet his father. He didn't know what he looked like because his mother didn't keep any pictures of him at home. Dustin hoped his father would look handsome and that he could see his future in his father's face. Dustin wished he would be a kind and caring father. But

most of all, he was nervous about his father
showing up at all. What if his father didn't
like him and never wanted to see him again?

He waited in the office with Mr. Lee for his
father. He shook his legs incessantly, and Mr.
Lee helped him take deep breaths. The phone
rang, and his therapist jumped to pick it up.
When he hung up, he said, "Well, Dustin,
your father is here. I'll go get him."

When the door opened again, he saw a
middle-aged, weather-beaten man behind
Mr. Lee. His hair was gray, uncombed, and
unruly. He wore a faded green shirt with
oily black stains and torn jeans. His face was
wrinkled and worn, but he had bright blue
eyes, and Dustin thought he saw tears welling
in the corners.

"Son, it's been so long … Let me look at
you," he said. "You've grown so much." He
came over to give him a hug.

"Please sit down," Mr. Lee said.

His father sat down next to him and continued to stare at him.

"Dustin, is there something you would like to say?" Mr. Lee asked.

They had prepared what he was going to say when he met his father. But no words came out. He could only look down to stop the tears from drowning him. *Why didn't you come earlier? Why did you abandon me?*

Mr. Lee took over the awkward silence. "Dustin did have many questions for you. But let him gather himself together first. Is there anything you would like to say to Dustin?"

His father did have a lot to say. He told them that he always wanted to see Dustin, but his mother always forbade it, and she even threatened to call the police if he came near. He said he thought about Dustin every day and sometimes went to the school playground to get a glimpse of his son. For a time, he had to go away, but even when he was a long distance away, he thought about his son daily.

"Why did you have to go away?" Dustin finally asked.

"It's hard to explain. Even if I could explain it, it's not something a child could understand," his father said.

Mr. Lee intervened. "Dustin is a lot smarter and more mature than you think. Why don't you try telling him anyway?"

"Well, hmm, I see. If he's anything like his mother, he would be very smart. Your mother … she is a remarkable woman," his dad said.

"Then why did you leave her? And me?" Dustin blurted out.

"We just weren't meant for each other. We fought all the time. I thought I loved her at one point, but I just …" His dad trailed off and became silent.

"Let me guess," Mr. Lee said softly. "You fell out of love with her?"

His father nodded.

"Did you try marriage counseling?" Mr. Lee asked.

"No. We did talk about it but never managed to get that far," Dustin's dad said. "I was just so tired of the constant nagging, the screaming, and her rage. I'm sorry, Dustin, that I had to leave you also. But I was so unhappy. I couldn't think clearly. All I knew was that I had to get out, or I would not survive." His father looked down and covered his face with his hands. His body shook, followed by a muffled cry. The tears dripped between his fingers and ran down his arms.

Mr. Lee handed him a box of tissues. They both waited in silence until his father could speak again.

His father dried his tears with the tissues

and opened his mouth to speak, but then the door opened. His mother came bursting into the door.

"Why don't you tell him why I made you leave?" she said, her voice low but wavering.

"How … why …" his father asked as he got up abruptly.

"Mom, I thought you were going to wait for me in the car," Dustin said.

"I knew he was going to lie to you. Make it sound like it was all my fault. I was listening through the door, and I couldn't stay outside any longer," she yelled. "Tell him what you did!" she screamed at his father.

"Wait a minute. Let's try to keep this civil," Mr. Lee said. "Please have a seat," he said to Dustin's mother.

She took a deep breath and sat down in the chair farthest away from them.

"Please, sit down again, sir," Mr. Lee said

to Dustin's father. His father sat down with a heavy sigh. Silence filled the room like a thick fog. They all looked at Mr. Lee to break the stillness.

"Okay, let's try this again without any screaming this time," Mr. Lee said. "Dustin's mother is clearly upset about something that happened in the past. Is this something we can talk about in front of Dustin? If not, would you want him to step outside?"

"No, I think he should hear what his father did to break up the family," his mother said, cold and motionless.

They all looked at his father, but he did not speak.

"Oh, now you don't have anything to say?" his mother snarled. "Should I tell him, then?"

"For God's sake, how many times do you want me to tell you 'I'm sorry'?" his father said. "You don't want to hear it anyway. I'm done." With that, he walked out of the room.

Mr. Lee went out of the room to follow him, perhaps to convince him to come back.

Did he just leave without saying goodbye? Dustin's heart sank.

His mother's voice broke through the silence. "I'm not surprised that he walked out," she said. "That's what he does, you know." Then she added, "Actually, you don't know since he was never there for you."

Mr. Lee came back without Dustin's father. He said, "He must have run quickly down the stairs. I couldn't see him anymore. I'm sorry, Dustin, I tried."

"That's why it's better that he stays away from us," his mother said. "You can't rely on him for anything. He is only going to hurt you like he hurt me."

"Mom, what did he do that hurt you so much?" Dustin asked. His mother was silent this time.

"*Mom*, what did he do?!" Dustin asked again.

She looked at Mr. Lee, and he nodded at her.

"He left us for another woman," she said, her voice breaking. "We weren't good enough for him."

***

Time passed slowly after the meeting with his father. After Dustin got over the initial shock, he cried for days. He didn't know if he would be able to see his father again. If he did, he didn't think he could ever forgive the man.

He also heard his mother's muffled cries in the next room. He didn't go back to see Mr. Lee during his usual time the following week. He started to wonder what the point of therapy was and why he should continue living at all. His thoughts started to slip back to the familiar dark place he had hoped to never revisit.

However, it was different this time. His mother had her own therapist, who supported her in pulling herself out of bed and getting Dustin back into therapy. At his mother's insistence, he went back to see Mr. Lee, who helped him through the trauma of his father's second abandonment. At times, Mr. Lee asked Dustin's mother to join Dustin for family sessions to discuss the implications of what she revealed at the meeting. His mother acknowledged that she made a mistake by bursting into the room and ruining any chance of healing between father and son. She was too consumed by her own pain and fury that she did not think of the consequences.

Eventually, Dustin was able to let go of his

anger against his mother. Mr. Lee said that forgiveness was more for Dustin's own sake than his mother's. Living with the anger and resentment was more harmful to his own mental and physical health.

Mr. Lee also recommended that Dustin see a child psychiatrist. He said that she might be able to recommend other treatment options, including medication. He said that she would only recommend medication as a last resort and only if his mom and Dustin were willing to try it.

PART TWO
LESSONS LEARNED FROM DUSTIN'S JOURNEY

At several points in Dustin's journey, a timely intervention could have changed the course of his life and his mother's for the better. In this section, I will share eleven lessons drawn from her mistakes. If you follow this guidance, you can improve the mental health of your child or teen. I will use quotes from the story as a lead-in to the lessons.

CHAPTER 1
LESSON 1: DON'T DO IT ALONE. ASK FOR HELP.

He did recall that his mother came to pick him up and argued with the teacher. Their heated exchange ended with his mother's tears, and she abruptly took his hand and dragged him out of the building. It was also the first time he saw her cry. Over the years, he saw her sob too many times. Sadness was her frequent companion.

Lesson 1: Don't do it alone. Ask for help. Dustin's mother was clearly overwhelmed with Dustin's disruptive behaviors, and she didn't know what to do. She only knew to react in anger and retreat into her sadness.

There are countless agencies online and in your local community that can offer support. NAMI (National Alliance on Mental Illness) is a national organization that offers mental health resources for adults as well as youths. You can reach the agency by visiting Nami.org, calling 1-800-950-6264, or texting "Helpline" to 62640. From there, you can ask for local community organizations that can provide guidance.

If Dustin's mother reached out to one of the centers or even asked his pediatrician to refer him to a local mental health center, Dustin could have had a better chance earlier in his life. Therapeutic preschool programs cater to emotionally challenged children in preschool years. I've helped many children who fit this category. The staff members in the therapeutic preschool program are trained to handle such children, and the kids often thrive in these programs.

Kelly was another patient who had

hyperactive problems ever since she could walk. Her mother said that she constantly climbed and jumped on furniture and had broken her bones several times. Kelly also had severe tantrums that lasted hours and resulted in property damage. Her mother admitted they had to replace the TV in the living room at least twice a year. Her mother couldn't keep a job since Kelly's preschool teachers would constantly call her to pick her up during the day. After several failed attempts to integrate Kelly into their preschool programs, the staff politely asked Kelly's mom not to bring her back. Kelly's mother was completely exhausted and overwhelmed by the time she brought Kelly to see me at the office.

Kelly qualified for the therapeutic preschool program due to her age and the severity of her symptoms. These programs are highly structured, and the staff are trained

to handle children who are hyperactive
and often aggressive. Kelly also qualified
for the service called Wrap Around at that
time (now called IBHS or Intensive Behavior
Health Service), which included several staff
members (a behavior specialist, a mobile
therapist, and one-to-one staff) who worked
with Kelly and her mother at home. Her
mother had little parenting experience, and
the behavior specialist had to practically train
her regarding the very basics of parenting.
The Wrap Around team also went to Kelly's
preschool to collaborate with her teachers.
With the support from these multiple
therapeutic staff members and changes to a
highly structured environment, Kelly was
able to thrive during the rest of her preschool
years.

The last time I saw them, Kelly was just
finishing second grade. Her mother beamed

with pride and told me that Kelly was getting good grades, and the teachers called her an "angel."

CHAPTER 2
LESSON 2: THE EARLIER, THE BETTER

He tried sitting in class quietly like the others, but a motor drove him from the inside that he couldn't calm. He tried raising his hand to answer his teacher, but words came out of his mouth that annoyed her, and she made him stand frequently in the corner. The other kids ridiculed and bullied him, so he fought to defend himself. Soon he was labeled as the troublemaker in his class, and nothing he did could change his title.

This description of Dustin is a classic example of someone who has ADHD (attention deficit hyperactivity disorder). People who don't believe in this disorder often blame these children as "not trying hard enough."

Imaging studies of the brain have revealed that the structure of these ADHD brains is different from the neurotypical brain. Research studies from Finland found that ADHD brains have reduced volume and gray matter differences in key areas that support cognitive functions such as memory and attention.[5]

Such studies reveal that ADHD children have different brain structures, and they are unable to control their impulses on their own. They need support and guidance from professionals who have experience in dealing with this condition. More imaging studies are still needed to give the public a better understanding of the ADHD disorder.

---

5 Roman-Urrestarazu, Andres. "Brain structural deficits and working memory fMRI dysfunction in young adults who were diagnosed with ADHD in adolescence." *European Child & Adolescent Psychiatry*, vol. 25, pp. 529–38.

Lesson 2: The earlier you get help for your child or teen, the better the outcome.
Dustin's plight was ignored not only by his mother but by his teacher as well. His teacher put him in a corner in order to teach him a lesson. She could not imagine that Dustin could have difficulty controlling his impulses due to key differences in his brain.

Teachers are often the first people to bring a youth's struggles to their parents. If the parents are open to suggestions, they will seek help immediately. Their children will have a better outcome since these youths will develop tools to manage their condition once properly treated.

Unfortunately, some parents choose to ignore the warnings. These children end up like Dustin, who become stigmatized for their challenges and ridiculed by their peers. I've seen some patients turn to extreme self-loathing, self-harm, and suicidal behaviors.

Dustin channeled his anger outward and fought with his aggressors. Unfortunately, children who get bullied like Dustin go on to become the worst bullies.

If Dustin's mother decided to get him help at a mental health center earlier, Dustin could have had a successful childhood. Professionals at mental health centers will always start with talk therapy first. Therapists will give children coping strategies to deal with their ADHD symptoms. If the youths do not improve after a period of talk therapy, only then will the therapist recommend an evaluation with a child psychiatrist. Medication is the last resort for children and adolescents and is undertaken with parental guidance.

CHAPTER 3
LESSON 3: MONITOR YOUR CHILD'S INTERNET USE

Even by third grade, he knew too much of the world since his mother left him with babysitters who were preoccupied with their phones. So, he roamed the Internet as freely as he wished. When his mother did come back from work, she often slept and stayed in her room.

On the Internet, he saw terrible things, especially regarding what men and women did to each other. There was so much violence that already existed and even more that people made up. He couldn't tear his eyes away from that brutality since he realized it excited him. He scoured the Internet, looking for more disturbing images and bloodshed, each time worse than the last. Was this how people normally treated each other or how they were supposed to behave? He also saw what people did to themselves, how they hurt themselves to deal with sadness.

Lesson 3: Monitor your child's internet use. In May 2023, the US Surgeon General, Vivek H. Murthy, released a new advisory about the effects of social media use on youth mental health.[6] Murthy noted that the use of social media has been an important driver of the youth mental health crisis. According to his report, adolescents who spend more than three hours on social media per day have double the risk of depression and anxiety.[7] Not only are they exposed to violent and sexual content, but they are also vulnerable

---

6 "Social Media and Youth Mental Health: The U.S. Surgeon General's Advisory." HHS.gov.

7 Riehm, Kira. "Associations Between Time Spent Using Social Media and Internalizing and Externalizing Problems Among US Youth." *JAMA psychiatry*, vol. 76, no. 12, 2019, 1266–73.

to cyberbullying. Social media use has also been cited as a reason for the increase in eating disorder rates among our youth due to propagating body dissatisfaction and low self-esteem.

The rise in tic-like behaviors in teenagers during the pandemic is an illustration of social media's clear and direct impact on our youth. During the pandemic, pediatricians and other pediatric subspecialists around the world noticed a marked increase in tic-like behaviors in children and adolescents. This sudden increase greatly puzzled the doctors until they found a correlation between the teens' tic-like behaviors and their consumption of Tourette's syndrome videos on social media such as TikTok.[8] Since their tic-like behaviors differed from Tourette's syndrome, the experts were

8 Vera, Alonso Zea. "The Phenomenology of Tics and Tic-Like Behavior in TikTok." *Pediatric Neurology*, vol. 130, 2020, pp. 14–20.

able to confirm that their tics were influenced by social media use.

Many parents believe that technology companies should play a greater role in supporting them to monitor the electronic use of their children. Smartphones come loaded with apps that can track our steps, our stocks, and the temperature of our houses. The iPhone has Screen Time, but it only tracks a limited amount of information. Children often find a way to turn it off so that parents are unable to track their actual usage. When I talk to parents about subscribing to a parental monitoring app, they often complain that they don't have the money and that the apps are not user-friendly. Why don't our smartphones come preloaded with an easy-to-use parental monitoring app that is childproof and does not require a subscription?

In the profit-driven market, cell phone

companies do not have the incentive to implement these changes since it will decrease their profit margins. Only with legislative enforcements could one ensure such protections.

In Jonathan Haidt's highly successful book, *The Anxious Generation*, he makes the argument that the radical change from a play-based childhood to a phone-based one has had a profound impact on our children and directly led to the current mental health crisis. His book has started discussions in various communities to implement the changes that he proposed. The staff at my children's school asked the parents to read *The Anxious Generation* and have a discussion about the book. After the conversation, the staff made policy changes at the school. The children are now required to put their phones away in their locker or a cell phone holder during instructional time.

CHAPTER 4
LESSON 4: BE VIGILANT

Even at that young age, he knew he was sad himself. He thought about his despondent mother, his worthless father, and the poverty they lived in. He only saw endless suffering that stretched before him, and he even thought about ending his life. Would his mother miss him if he died? Or would it add to her sadness? He thought about the rope in the closet and how easy it would be to tie it around his neck and end the anguish. He took it out to touch its roughness. He went so far as to feel its tightness around his neck.

Lesson 4: Be vigilant.
The first sign of depression in children is often different from adults. Depressed children

can have frequent outbursts and disruptive behaviors in school since they are unable to verbalize their anguish.

On several occasions, I had to be the first person to tell the parent/guardian that their child had contemplated suicide or made a serious attempt. In Dustin's case, he told me that he had thought about hanging himself many years ago and almost attempted it. He had never told a single soul before, but he was glad to get it off his chest when he finally talked about it.

For people who have seriously contemplated suicide, like Dustin, calling the national suicide hotline 988 could have been helpful. If one does not want to talk to a counselor on the phone, they can also text 988, and a trained crisis counselor will text them back.

Dustin had been meaning to tell his

therapist and his mother about his near
suicide attempt, but he just couldn't bring
himself to talk about it after lying to them
initially. At the very first meeting with the
therapist, Mr. Lee had asked him about any
current or past suicidal ideations or attempts,
and Dustin said no because he was afraid that
Mr. Lee would send him to the hospital. Even
after developing trust with Mr. Lee, he could
not bring himself to tell him that he lied about
such an important detail in the beginning. By
the time he came to see me, he was ready to
tell someone about it. Once he told me, the
floodgates opened up.

CHAPTER 5
LESSON 5: BE PART OF A COMMUNITY

He couldn't kill himself because of the voice of his grandmother in his head. She was the only one he could remember who showed kindness and affection in his life. She cuddled him to sleep when he had nightmares. She bandaged his knees when he skinned them and kissed them to heal faster. She told him about a place a person went after death, only if he made good choices. She took him to church and taught him more about the place beyond death. He wanted to make good choices because he loved his grandmother, but he still couldn't control his impulses that were always one step ahead of him.

He was devastated when his grandmother died from COVID-19. The doctors tried to save

Grandma, but she continued fading away. He went to see her in the hospital only to see tubes coming out of her in all directions. His grandmother reached for him and told him to be brave and good, so she could see him in heaven one day.

Lesson 5: Be part of a community.
Dustin's grandmother took him to church and told him about the place beyond death. Her message of hope might have saved Dustin's life. It's estimated that 80 percent of the people in the world belong to a religious community. Many people are born into a particular faith and find comfort and safety in the rituals of their belief system. Some people seek meaning greater than themselves and find answers from a particular religious group. Joining a community of like-minded believers can have many mental health benefits. By connecting with people you can

call on socially or during times of crisis, you are more likely to preserve your sanity while dealing with your troubled youth.

If you don't want to join a religious group, join a different type of community. NAMI (which was mentioned in an earlier chapter) has a family support group. The LiveWell Foundation (tel: 267-530-3739) provides free depression groups for teens, adults, and seniors. These groups are available in person and on Zoom.

Bereavement groups are available at some hospitals. If you want to join a bereavement group after losing a loved one, your local hospital might have one. Some bereavement groups meet on Zoom also. If you want to receive only online support, Grieving.com is one of the oldest grief support communities on the Internet.

CHAPTER 6
LESSON 6: FIX YOURSELF FIRST

His mother yelled, threatened, and even begged him to stop the havoc since she had already lost several jobs. However, he couldn't calm the storm that raged inside him, no matter how hard he tried. His teachers asked his mother to get him some help so that he could quiet his mind. They told her that there was a name for his anguish, and once named, he could start the healing process. However, his mother ignored their pleas because she was afraid of those institutions that asked questions and judged her. She knew deep down that she was at fault for her son's anguish, and it was easier to bury her guilt and hide her shame rather than expose herself. She would rather deal with the constant barrage of complaints from the school than be forced to examine her own broken soul.

Lesson 6: Fix yourself first before hoping to fix your kid.

As parents/guardians, we have our own baggage that we carry with us as we try to raise our children to be "perfect little angels." Up to a certain age, children look up to us and absorb every one of our idiosyncrasies and often adopt them as their own. If you are suffering from a mental health problem of your own, don't delay getting treatment for yourself.

On the plane, the flight attendants will tell you that if the oxygen masks come down, you have to put the mask on yourself first before you can help others. If you try to help with your child's mask first, you will pass out before you finish. It's important that you are well-oxygenated and conscious in order to help others around you.

Similarly, if you are depressed yourself, it's hard to think clearly and make the right decisions for your child.

Many parents have given me excuses as to why they couldn't get mental health treatment for themselves. They cited problems with their insurance, lack of time, difficulty with transportation, etc. One parent outright told me that they were afraid of what they would find out about themselves if they started therapy. It's important to put these fears aside and start therapy for yourself if you have your own problems. Children are like sponges and will adopt your maladaptive habits unconsciously if you don't make efforts to change them.

CHAPTER 7
LESSON 7: IF THERE IS A WILL, THERE IS A WAY

Lesson 7: If there is a will, there is a way.
Jason's mother was a victim of domestic violence. During the pandemic in 2020, cases of domestic violence rose 25 to 33 percent globally, according to the *American Journal of Emergency Medicine.*[9]

When I first met Jason, I saw him and his mother on a small video screen at home since my office was closed due to the pandemic lockdown. During my first encounter with him, he appeared distraught and hesitant with his answers. Initially, I thought it was due to

---

9 Boserup, Brad. "Alarming trends in US domestic violence during the COVID-19 pandemic." *The American Journal of Emergency Medicine*, vol. 38, no. 12, 2020, pp. 2753–55.

the poor quality of the video.

Jason was referred to me due to his severe anger outbursts and anxiety. Toward the end of the video call, he revealed that he had witnessed a domestic violence incident between his parents shortly before his appointment. At first, his mother tried to downplay the severity of the abuse, but she ended up admitting that Jason's father did hit her in front of the children, and she couldn't take it anymore. She had also lost her mother to COVID-19, and she was still reeling from the loss.

Jason's mother wanted to leave Jason's father, but she didn't have any financial means, and she felt stuck. I gave her resources to obtain support so she could leave the abusive situation. I also encouraged her to obtain therapy for herself. At first, she gave me the same excuse I heard from many parents. Lack of time and insurance problems were on the top of her list. However, I told her to give it time to think about it, and she agreed.

Last time I saw Jason and his mother, they had moved out of the father's house. With guidance from our agency's support staff, his mother was able to gather resources to move out. She also filed a restraining order against Jason's father so that he could not retaliate.

Jason's mother even started therapy for herself. She said it took a long time to find an agency that would accept her insurance, but she persisted and found one. During the pandemic, many agencies were overwhelmed with an influx of patients and stopped accepting new people. She told me that she knew it was important to put the oxygen mask on herself before she could help her son.

Once Jason moved out of the miserable

environment, he thrived. He stopped having violent outbursts and focused on his studies. He received *A*'s and *B*'s, and his mother received praise from his teachers. Jason even took the initiative to help around the house.

CHAPTER 8
LESSON 8: FIND THE RIGHT BALANCE

His thoughts started to slip back to the familiar dark place he had hoped to never revisit. However, it was different this time. His mother had her own therapist, who supported her in pulling herself out of bed and getting Dustin back into therapy. At his mother's insistence, Dustin went back to see Mr. Lee, who helped him through the trauma of his father's second abandonment.

Lesson 8: Find the right balance. Be supportive but firm with boundaries. Before meeting Mr. Lee, Dustin's mother mainly provided physical necessities for Dustin, but she did not know how to meet his emotional needs. With guidance from Mr.

Lee, she gradually learned skills to become a loving mother.

Parenting is one of the most difficult skills to learn in the world. Even though countless books have been written to help parents navigate this tricky subject, I have not met one person who can claim that they have mastered it, including myself. In fact, I will be the first one to admit that I've made many mistakes as a parent. However, many parents will tell you that they strive to find the right balance between giving their child wholehearted support and firm boundaries.

Andrew is another patient who was a college student at the time of this writing. Last time I saw him, his father beamed with pride. His mother had abandoned them when he was three years old, and he struggled with her absence. He threatened to kill himself at school, and he was hospitalized at age ten for his own safety. He recalled feeling isolated and depressed at the time. When he finally left the hospital and went back to school, he struggled to catch up.

Social interactions were always difficult for him. He had problems maintaining eye contact and making friends. He often came home empty-handed from the corner store because he had anxiety attacks before going up to the cash register to interact with the store clerk.

Andrew was diagnosed with autism and attended a social interaction group that was instrumental in improving his social skills. During our latest encounter, he told me that he still used the techniques he had learned from the autism group, such as maintaining eye contact and reading people's faces.

Andrew's father suffered from multiple medical problems and physical limitations, but he was one of the most supportive parents I encountered. He was with him at every appointment, and he made sure they came on time. He also kept in touch with his teachers at school and addressed any issues as soon as they arose.

Andrew also had an older sister who was like a mother to him. The sister took him out to exercise together at the gym and made sure Andrew and their father were well taken care of. Despite the loneliness and isolation Andrew experienced at school, he always knew he had a loving family that he could rely on.

On the subject of support, we cannot ignore the catastrophic rise in suicide rates among LGBTQ teens during the pandemic. Stigmatization, victimization, and alienation were among the key factors that contributed to their increase in depression and anxiety.

According to the Trevor Project's 2022 national survey on LGBTQ youth mental health, 45 percent of transgender and nonbinary youths seriously considered suicide, and 14 percent attempted suicide. It was estimated that these teens were more than four times more likely to attempt suicide than their heterosexual peers. However, the LGBTQ teens who received high social support from their families attempted suicide at less than half the rate compared to those receiving low to moderate support.[10]

Being supportive doesn't mean allowing your child or teen to do whatever they want. It's important to set boundaries and let your child know that they should not cross them. Having a curfew or giving limited time on electronics (especially on a school night) is one

10 "2022 National Survey on LGBTQ Youth Mental Health." The Trevor Project, https://www.thetrevorproject.org/survey-2022/.

example of a clear boundary. Communicate clearly what the consequences will be if they cross the boundary, and make sure you follow through. If you don't, your child/teen won't take you seriously.

CHAPTER 9
LESSON 9: YOU ARE THE PARENT, NOT THEIR FRIEND

Lesson 9: You are their parent, not their friend.

It's often easy to believe that by loving our children, we develop a friendship with them. But there is a difference between being "friendly" with them and being their friend. As a friend, they might feel that you are on equal ground with them, and thus, they will treat you with less respect.

I often tell parents that the most important job in the world is to be the best parent for their child. Their children will have many friends who come and go, but their parents will be with them for life.

Melissa had a very permissive parent who

allowed her to do "whatever" she wanted.
Her mom would allow her to come home
anytime she wanted and never took her phone
away. While interviewing Melissa alone, I
thought she would tell me she had it made.
However, that was not the case. She said that
all her friends' parents gave them rules, but
her mother never gave any, and she perceived
it as a lack of love. She said she wished her
mother, Jenna, had been stricter and had
given her some more guidelines, since she
never developed any discipline for herself.
Even though it was not what I expected, I
wasn't completely shocked. From Jenna's
perspective, she thought she was being a
"cool" mother by giving Melissa all the
freedom in the world. Jenna had strict parents
while she was growing up, so she wanted
the opposite for her daughter. She thought
Melissa would grow up to be a happier

person than she was. However, that was not the case. Melissa was just as miserable as her mother at the same age.

CHAPTER 10
LESSON 10: ASK FOR FORGIVENESS

At times, Mr. Lee asked Dustin's mother to join Dustin for family sessions to discuss the implications of what she revealed at the meeting. His mother acknowledged that she made a mistake by bursting into the room and ruining any chance of healing between father and son. She was too consumed by her own pain and fury that she did not think of the consequences.

As more time passed, Dustin was able to let go of his anger against his mother. Mr. Lee said that forgiveness was more for Dustin's own sake than his mother's. Living with the anger and resentment would be more harmful for his own mental and physical health.

Lesson 10: Don't let pride get in your way. If you made a mistake, ask for forgiveness. There is not one parent in this world who didn't make a mistake raising their child. No parent/guardian has been able to reach the perfect balance every single time. If you know you made a mistake, it's important to acknowledge it and ask for forgiveness.

Lynn and her father came to see me due to Lynn's depression and self-harm. They had undergone intensive family therapy, but they were at an impasse. Lynn finally told me that her father had made many negative comments over the years, especially about her weight, and it had hurt her. I talked to her father alone and told him what Lynn said (with Lynn's permission). At first, he was baffled as to why it should bother her, since he only "teased" her about her weight, and he thought she knew that it was only a "joke." Besides, that was the way his own parents jabbed at him, so he interacted with his children in a similar manner. He did admit that the negative comments from his parents did hurt him at times, but he was able to "get over it." I asked him how he would feel if his parents asked his forgiveness for the criticisms that had especially hurt him.

"I don't know … I guess I would have felt better … I will never know since both of them passed away," he said.

After our discussion, Lynn's father had a long talk with Lynn about his mistakes and asked her for forgiveness. Lynn was able to open up to her father about all the past wounds she received from him that were particularly difficult to overcome. That talk was the beginning of their healing journey together.

CHAPTER 11
LESSON 11: BE FLEXIBLE, KEEP AN OPEN MIND

Mr. Lee also recommended that Dustin see a child psychiatrist. He said that she might be able to recommend other treatment options, including medication. He said that she would only recommend medication as a last resort and only if his mom and Dustin were willing to try it.

Lesson 11: Be flexible. Keep an open mind. By the time Dustin came to see me, he had made progress in many aspects of his life. His relationship with his mother had improved, and he had begun to overcome the trauma from his father's abandonment. He didn't feel sad anymore, and he had stopped having suicidal thoughts. However, he still suffered

from the inner "motor" that drove him, and
he had trouble concentrating, which resulted
in poor academic performance. Dustin's
mother felt that they had tried everything else
and came to me as a last resort.

According to the MTA (Multimodal
Treatment of ADHD) multisite study,
treatment with medication alone and
treatment with medication and therapy are
significantly superior to intensive behavior
therapy alone.[11] When I explain this study
to my patients, I tell them that therapy alone
isn't enough for ADHD. Treatment with
medication alone and medication along with
therapy were found to be more helpful. In my
experience, the combination of medication

11 The MTA Cooperative Group. "A 14-month randomized clinical
trial of treatment strategies for attention-deficit/hyperactivity disorder.
The MTA Cooperative Group. Multimodal Treatment Study of Children
with ADHD." *Archives of General Psychiatry*, vol. 56, no. 12, 1999,
pp. 1073–86.

and therapy has been most effective. However, many parents have misgivings about giving psychiatric medications to their children. When a parent is able to honestly discuss their hesitancy, I tell them that it's absolutely normal. In fact, I am wary of parents who do not have any apprehensions about giving their child medications.

I had the experience of riding on the school bus with my daughter while going on her school field trip as a chaperone. During the bus trip back, I struck up a conversation with one of the other chaperones on the bus. She was a medical professional, but even she had doubts about trying psychiatric medications for her child. Her daughter had a long trial of therapy for her severe anxiety, but they did not see any improvements. They were wavering about trying an anti-anxiety medication.

"It's perfectly normal to have these doubts," I said. "But I tell my patients and their families to keep an open mind. If you tried everything else, what do you have to lose by trying medication? If it doesn't work, you can always stop it. But you have to give it a fair amount of time. For depression and anxiety medications, you have to give it at least four to six weeks to see any improvements, and the progress is very gradual. For ADHD meds, you can see the difference almost right away if you find the right med and the right dose. Some people do get side effects, but they can be minimized by working with the doctor. "

The next time I saw her, she told me that she went ahead and tried an anxiety medication for her child. She was glad that she did since her daughter had made significant improvements. I was glad to hear that she had opened her mind and taken my advice.

When I saw Dustin and his mother, I also told them to keep an open mind about medication. They said they would consider it and let me know at the next visit.

Just before they left, his mother said, "Thank you for your help. It's been a long and difficult road, and I know we have a longer path ahead."

"You're welcome," I said. "I hope you keep yourselves on that path."

"Oh, yes, we will," she said. "Don't you worry about us. We'll take it day by day. And when things get tough, I try to imagine the day when Dustin thanks me and tells me that it was all worth it in the end. That's what keeps me going."

PART THREE
RECOGNIZING THE WARNING SIGNS; TAKE EFFECTIVE ACTION

What do you do if you walk in on your child in the middle of a suicide attempt? In Dustin's case, the memory of his grandmother stopped him from completing the suicide, and he continued to live for a better day. But not everyone is so lucky.

Over the years, I have met many parents who found their children in various stages of suicidal ideation to attempts. They came to me baffled by their children's actions and asked what steps to take or if they could have done anything more. In the following chapters, I will give examples of some scenarios and recommend a course of action in each case. Please note that the scenarios are only possible outcomes, and they can vary depending on the situation.

CHAPTER 1
VALERIE: SUICIDAL IDEATION TO ATTEMPT AND SELF-HARM

Valerie was a straight-A student and the captain of her volleyball team. She was also in the popular crowd, and her "friends" thought she had it all. But Valerie could not live up to the pressure of perfection. Her parents were going through a divorce, and she found herself crying every night. She had thoughts about ending her life. Initially, she didn't think she had the "guts" to kill herself. But the thoughts became intense as her sadness persisted, and she started to think about taking pills to end her life. She knew where the painkiller (Tylenol, Ibuprofen) bottles were kept and where the knives were in the kitchen. She snuck down to the kitchen in the middle of the night and hid the knife in her room. She held the knife and scratched her wrist with it night after night, but she could not bring herself to deeply slit her wrist due to the thoughts of her family and friends.

What would happen to her parents and her younger sister? What about her boyfriend, Jake?

She decided that she didn't really want her life to end but just wanted the unrelenting misery to stop.

The next day at school, she told Jake about her near attempt to end her life. He listened carefully and comforted her. He was shocked by her confession and realized he had to make a choice. Should he keep her secret, or should he tell a trusted adult to handle the matter? He was initially scared of losing Valerie and kept quiet. But he could not contain the guilt. Her death would be his fault if he didn't speak up. He hated to do it, but he went to talk to a school counselor about what Valerie told him. He would rather see Valerie mad but alive than the alternative. Besides, there might come a day when Valerie would thank him for speaking up.

The counselor immediately called Valerie's mother about what Jake told her. Her mother was speechless over the phone. *Did the counselor call the right parent? Just that morning, she had been laughing and joking with her sister before she went to school. That can't be right ...*

"Hello, hello, are you still there?" the counselor said over the phone, but Valerie's mother, Jennifer, only heard a faint whisper over the thumping of her heart.

"What ...? How ...?" were the only words she could muster through her parched lips. Tears streaked down her face and pooled under her chin.

"Mrs. Warner, did you hear me? I said you have to come to the counseling office and pick up Valerie," the counselor persisted.

"Um … um … okay, I'll be there as soon as I can," Jennifer said as she hung up.

On the drive to school, Jennifer went over millions of scenarios in her head. Most of it was scanning her past to consider what she had missed or what she had done wrong. At that point, I would have advised her to stop focusing on the past and prepare for the future. Time for reflection would come later, and it would not help anyone if she reacted hysterically. The best course of action would be to keep calm and comply with the recommendations given by the school counselor since she has the knowledge and experience to handle such situations.

Jennifer was able to calm down and compose herself by the time she arrived at

the school to pick up Valerie. She could see
that Valerie was scared but also relieved that
the truth had come out. The counselor, Mrs.
Thomas, was a kind woman who listened and
spoke patiently about what Valerie shared
and the next steps that would be required.

Scenario 1:
If the counselor believed that the child was no
longer in any danger, she could recommend
that the youth enroll in a school-based mental
health program such as IBHS (Intensive
Behavior Health Service), if the school had
such a program. It would take time to enroll
in this program, but once a child did so, they
would start therapy with a mobile therapist at
school. The mobile therapist could also go to
the child's house and have sessions with the
parents/guardians. The IBHS program staff
could also recommend a behavior specialist

and one-to-one staff to accompany the child at school, if warranted. However, the one-to-one staff is usually recommended for children who are severely aggressive and need constant supervision at school.

If the school did not have such a program, the counselor could recommend an evaluation at a nearby mental health clinic for the child to start therapy as soon as possible. However, these places can have long wait times.

Scenario 2:

If the counselor was unsure of the child's safety, she would recommend that the child be evaluated by a psychiatrist at a psychiatric crisis center, if there was one in the area. If not, the counselor would recommend that the child be taken to an emergency room for an evaluation.

If there is a behavioral urgent care center

(UCC) nearby, this would be another place
that the counselor could recommend. This
is the equivalent of an urgent care clinic that
would not treat people in a serious emergency
but rather those who would need immediate
treatment for a minor to moderate problem.
In the UCC, Valerie and her mother could
talk to a mental health professional who
would assess Valerie's safety and make
recommendations for treatment.

Scenario 3:
If the counselor determined that Valerie was
still in danger, she would ask the guardian to
take her directly to a psychiatric crisis center
or emergency room. I've had children tell
me that they overdosed on pills but woke
up the next day and went to school. In cases
like this, the guardian would need to take the
child to the emergency room for a full medical

evaluation. In the ER, the medical staff would check vitals and labs and "pump" the stomach if needed.

If the vitals are unstable and the doctor sees abnormal values on the bloodwork, the child would be sent to the medical unit for observation. Since the child was admitted for a suicide attempt, a one-to-one staff member would be sitting next to the child to ensure safety at all times. If the child becomes medically cleared, a psychiatrist would be called to talk to the child and the guardian about the attempt. Depending on what the psychiatrist finds during the evaluation, the family would be given a set of instructions to follow in regard to treatment. Some of these recommendations might vary depending on what type of facilities are available in your area.

Recommendation 1:

The psychiatrist will recommend that the
youth stay at a psychiatric inpatient unit
if the attempt was serious enough. This
will be a locked unit to maintain safety, so
that another attempt will not be made. The
psychiatric staff will also conduct therapy
(group, individual) and family meetings,
and sometimes family therapy, during the
child's stay. The psychiatrist at the unit might
recommend medication, if needed, after a
discussion with the guardian and the youth.
Depending on the state, teens can consent to
their own psychiatric medication, but they are
often encouraged to obtain support from their
parents since the parents will need to safely
monitor their medications after discharge. In
the state of Pennsylvania, the age of consent is
fourteen.

Most people fear going to a locked unit,

but some children told me that it was helpful because they gained valuable insights during their time in the hospital unit. Some of them were just happy to get a second chance at life, and others were thankful to learn coping skills and life lessons from the unit.

Recommendation 2:

If the psychiatrist determines that the child was not in danger and that their action was only a "cry for help," but the youth is still in need of an intense period of therapy, they will recommend partial hospitalization.

A partial hospital is a place where a child goes all day for therapy instead of going to school, for a period of two weeks to a month. Usually, a van will come pick them up around 9:00 a.m. and drop them back home around 3:00 p.m. so the youth can sleep at home.

The parent/guardian will need to tell the

school staff that the child was admitted to
the partial hospitalization program, so that
teachers can give them schoolwork to do
during their absence. At the partial hospital,
the child will be required to attend individual
and group therapy sessions. There will be
time for the child to complete the schoolwork
so they don't fall behind in school. Family
meetings and sessions will be requested by
the hospital staff to discuss any issues that
come up during their stay.

A psychiatrist will evaluate the child in the
partial hospital for any need for medication,
if appropriate. If medication is recommended,
the psychiatrist will have a discussion with
the parent and the youth before starting any
meds.

Recommendation 3:
If the psychiatrist determines that the child is

safe enough to go home and attend outpatient therapy once a week at an office, then the child will be sent home. The medical staff will give a list of mental health clinic locations nearby, and the guardian will need to call them and make an appointment as soon as possible. When the parent calls, it is helpful to let the staff know that their child was recently in the ER or the crisis center so they can be moved up on a priority list, if the clinic has one.

If the child already has a therapist, they are recommended to see their therapist as soon as possible after discharge.

In Valerie's case, the psychiatrist at the ER decided that Valerie's near attempt was a "cry for help" because she did not go through with slitting her wrist and told her boyfriend about the attempt the next day. The boyfriend made the correct choice to tell the school counselor in order to start the chain of events so that Valerie could start the healing process. In the end, Valerie did thank her boyfriend for speaking up.

Depending on the psychiatrist in the ER, they could also recommend that Valerie attend a partial hospitalization program. Although she did not go through with slitting her wrist, she had engaged in self-harm by "scratching" herself with a knife countless times, and she would benefit from intensive therapy to prevent her from engaging in self-harm and suicidal gestures again. Valerie would go home and wait for the partial hospital staff to call them when a space was available for her to start.

Self-Harm
Self-harm, or SIB (self-injurious behavior), is a tricky subject in psychiatry. Some

patients insist that they engaged in self-harm
(especially cutting) due to emotional pain
but would never think to kill themselves.
They say that the physical pain from the cuts
distracts them from the emotional distress at
the moment. However, the scars of the cut
remind them of what they did, and they feel
worse afterward. Because they feel worse,
they engage in the cutting to mute the pain.
So, the cycle continues. If this is not treated
properly, the patient can get highly addicted
to the physical pain.

Some patients admit that they did think
about cutting deep and ending their life when
they engaged in self-harm. However, they
decided to keep the cuts at a superficial level
since they realized they didn't really want to
die. They like to toy with the idea of dying,
but deep down, they know they can't and
won't kill themselves.

However, self-harm is a "slippery slope."
A patient might have started off as cutting
superficially to mute the emotional pain, but
the distress could be so unbearable that they
end up cutting deeper than they intended. If
they end up cutting the "wrong" spot, they
could bleed out quickly and end their life. So,
these patients should be evaluated and treated
carefully.

Valerie attended the partial program as
recommended by the psychiatrist in the ER.
She rode a van to the building, where she
met other children who experienced similar
problems she had. She attended the individual
sessions with her therapist, who helped her
gain insight into her negative patterns and
find coping strategies to improve. She also
participated in group sessions and shared her
issues with others and listened to the concerns
and tragedies of her peers. During one of

the groups, she met Damion, who shared his traumatic experiences living with drug-addicted parents. Valerie knew she shouldn't compare herself to others, but she started to appreciate her parents, who adored her despite the problems they were having with each other. She also loved her younger sister and didn't want her to follow in her footsteps. By the time she was discharged from the partial program, Valerie was ready to take on the world.

CHAPTER 2
DAMION: TRAUMA AND ABUSE

When Damion was six years old, he witnessed his father pointing a gun to his mother's head. His mother was already black and blue from his father's drunken beating, and he pleaded for her life. His older brother was seventeen years old at the time, and he called the cops. He remembered the two policemen standing in their living room and handcuffing his father. They took him away in the police car, and he remembered feeling relieved that the monster was gone.

He also recalled his mother snorting powders up her nose and injecting needles into her arms. His father did the same things before he went away, so he thought they were normal adult activities. But Damion didn't like that his mother was constantly sleeping on the sofa and didn't make sure they had enough to eat. His brother was always out with his friends, but he came home at night to give him donuts or half-eaten pizza. He later found out that his brother waited by the trash can at Dunkin Donuts to dig out the unsold donuts. When his brother didn't come home for days, he was so hungry that he went to his neighbor to ask for food.

The neighbor was a kind lady who lived down the street. Her eyes widened when Damion asked for food, but she invited him to come in the house and gave him as much food as he could stuff in his mouth. The neighbor also gave Damion warm clothes to wear and food to take home. The next thing he remembered was a man entering their house to talk to his mother and taking Damion away from home.

Damion lived in six different foster homes for eight years until he returned to his sober mother. During this time, Damion was sexually and physically abused by multiple men and women from the various foster homes. He was afraid to tell anyone because they would often threaten to kill him if he said anything. (I would like to point out that not all children who end up in the foster care system have such horrible experiences. Many, if not most, children live with loving foster families and become adopted or return to their family of origin.)

By the time Damion came back to his mother's house at age fourteen, he was not the same six-year-old that his mother knew. He was aggressive and would often yell, scream, and hit her with the smallest provocation. He woke up with nightmares every night and couldn't go back to sleep. He refused to go to school on most days, and when he did go to school, he often fought with his peers.

One day, when his mother asked him to clean his room, Damion got into such a rage that he picked up the living room TV and threw it at his mother. He didn't stop with the TV but threw whatever he could grab in the living room.

If Damion lives in an area that has a mobile crisis team, his mother could call them for support during a crisis. Most mobile crisis phone lines are open 24/7, and they have staff that can come to the house to talk to the troubled youth. They can also connect the family with resources to follow up for ongoing support.

If you aren't sure if a mobile crisis team is available in your area, you can call or text 988 (national suicide and crisis line) to ask for help. If Damion did not have a mobile crisis team in his area, and the mother felt her own life was in danger, she could call the police as a last resort.

Damion's mother called 988 and received support to call the mobile crisis team in their neighborhood. By the time the crisis staff arrived at the house, Damion had calmed down. The team sat down with Damion and his mother to give them simple coping strategies. They also gave his mother some numbers to call for Damion to start therapy at a local mental health center.

At the clinic, his therapist recommended TF-CBT (trauma-focused cognitive behavioral therapy) to address the trauma of his abandonment and abuse. TF-CBT is a structured twelve-to-sixteen sessions therapy that involves the child and a non-offending caregiver (safe adult who did not inflict the violence) in order to support the trauma victim by using cognitive behavior techniques and gradual exposure. Cognitive behavior techniques involve identifying inaccurate thoughts of the trauma and developing coping skills to improve the youth's behavior. Exposure involves gradually reminding the individual of the specifics of trauma (places, people, memories) so that they can reduce distress and decrease trauma-related reactions. TF-CBT is effective in treating PTSD (post-traumatic stress disorder) and meets high levels of evidence.[12]

---

12 Ramirez de Arellano, Michael A. "Trauma-Focused Cognitive-Behavioral Therapy for Children and Adolescents: Assessing the Evidence." *Psychiatric Services*, vol. 65, no. 5, 2014, pp. 591–602.

CHAPTER 3
AVA: VICTIM OF A BULLY AND EATING DISORDER

Ava loved to eat. Her grandmother baked the best cookies, and she often went over to visit her after school. She also indulged in chips and sodas that were readily available at her house. Her parents and relatives often expressed their love by giving her food, so she also ate in order to please them. Her mother described her as a "happy" child and a "perfect little angel" before she started grade school.

Once she started school, her classmates relentlessly teased and bullied her for her large size. She was also taller than her peers, so they often called her the "whale." She hated the nickname and often cried when she came home. Mornings were difficult for everyone since Ava cried and pleaded to stay home, and the parents constantly struggled to get her ready for school. She was often late for her classes, and her grades suffered.

Her parents went to her school and met with various school staff to stop the bullying, but it didn't help.

Bullying is defined as physical, verbal, and relational aggression due to a power imbalance. Three types of bullying exist: physical bullying (hitting, kicking), verbal bullying (teasing, taunting), and social bullying (spreading rumors, embarrassing someone).

Schools have anti-bullying campaigns to raise awareness, but they are not always effective for all subgroups of children. Studies showed that the anti-bullying interventions (KiVa, NoTrap!, Olweus Bullying Prevention

Program, and ViSC) reduced bullying perpetration by 19 to 20 percent and victimization by 15 to 16 percent.

These school-based anti-bullying programs were reported to benefit children who had high initial victimization compared to low victimization before the intervention. They also helped children in the younger (less than twelve years old) group compared to the older adolescent group.[13]

Among adolescents, "informal peer involvement" or "encouraging bystanders" was found to be effective. These programs taught peers to speak up against the bully and support the victims. Although most students disapproved of the bullying, studies showed that only 10 to 25 percent of peers reached out

13 Hensums, Maud. "What Works for Whom in School-Based Anti-bullying Interventions? An Individual Participant Data Meta-analysis." *Prev Sci*, vol. 24, no. 8, 2023, 1435–46.

to help the victims.[14]

By encouraging prosocial behaviors such as direct defending (publicly confronting the bullies) and indirect defending (comforting the victim or asking an adult for help privately), some of these programs resulted in a decrease in bullying behavior.

How should parents and guardians respond when a child comes to them about a bully? First, make sure to respond appropriately. I've heard several children tell me that they told their parents about getting bullied, but they were mostly ignored. They were told that "it's not that bad," and that, "it's part of growing up," and that they should learn to deal with it on their own. These children can end up feeling helpless

14 Trach, J. "Bystander responses to school bullying: A cross-sectional investigation of grade and sex differences." *Canadian Journal of School Psychology*, vol. 25, 2010, pp. 114–130.

and hopeless, which are signs of depression. If a more serious life-threatening situation came up, they might not go to their parents for help.

On the other extreme, some parents react with severe anger and hysteria. They will call the school staff and yell at them over the phone or at a school meeting. This kind of approach is also not helpful because it can produce hostility from the school staff.

The best approach would be to stay calm and give your child assurance that you will do everything you can to protect them.

After gathering the facts and assessing the severity, ask the school staff (teacher, school counselor) to intervene on your child's behalf.

If there is no action, you can escalate it to the administration (principal first, then the school superintendent) for help. If you aren't satisfied with their response, contact your state's representative or your state's department of education. State laws should also protect your child. You can find your state's laws and policies against bullying at the Stopbullying.gov website.

The URL for this page is www. stopbullying.gov/resources/laws.

If it's cyberbullying, save the evidence, such as screenshots, emails, and text messages. The parent/guardian will need to report the cyberbullying to the social media websites and the internet service provider. Some states consider cyberbullying a crime, especially if a threat of violence or pornography is involved. Again, check the Stopbullying.gov website to see if your state law applies.

***

Ava withdrew to her room as soon as she

came home. When she came out of her room, she was often tired and irritable. Her parents noticed that she was skipping meals. Even when she did eat with them, she barely touched her food. One day, her mother caught her binging on junk food and running to the bathroom to throw up.

Her parents brought her to see me because they were concerned that she had developed an eating disorder. During the evaluation, Ava constantly shook her legs and gave very little eye contact. She was slightly overweight and wore a large hoodie and baggy jeans to cover her body even though the temperature was 90 degrees Fahrenheit outside. She spoke at a slow rate with a very low volume. She gave short answers to my questions but kept a respectful tone.

I diagnosed Ava with bulimia nervosa, which is a type of eating disorder

characterized by binging and compensatory
behaviors such as self-induced vomiting,
along with misuse of laxatives and
medications to lose weight. Depending
on the frequency and the severity of the
compensatory behaviors, it's a potentially
life-threatening condition since it can lead to
irregular heartbeat and even heart failure. If
someone with this condition doesn't drink
enough fluids, the dehydration can lead to
kidney failure. They often develop tooth
decay and gum disease, along with sores and
scars on the knuckles of their hands.

Since Ava's eating disorder had only
begun recently and it had not been severe,
I recommended that Ava start with talk
therapy first. Ava was referred to a center
that specializes in helping children with
eating disorders. Once she was assessed at
the center, she started individual therapy and

family therapy. Her parents also called their state's Department of Education, and the staff found an advocate for the family to support them at school. Soon the bullying stopped, and Ava felt safe to go to school daily.

Ava was also diagnosed with depression and anxiety. Her parents saw little improvement after she had six months of therapy, so they asked me about starting her on medication. For children and adolescents with depression and/or anxiety, SSRIs (selective serotonin reuptake inhibitors) are the first line of medications to consider. They include medications such as Zoloft, Prozac, and Lexapro. Often, the parents will choose the medication that was effective for a family member. In Ava's case, her mother had a bout of depression during her adolescent years, and Lexapro was helpful, so the parents asked if Ava could start Lexapro.

After checking Ava's bloodwork to rule out medical conditions such as anemia or thyroid problems that could contribute to depression and anxiety, Ava started with the lowest dose of Lexapro at 5 mg. After four to six weeks, Ava didn't feel any difference on the medication. Therefore, it was increased to 10 mg for another four to six weeks. After starting the Lexapro 10 mg, Ava told her mother that she felt less tired and less nervous about going to school. Her mother noticed that Ava smiled more often and came out of her room to watch TV with the rest of the family. During this time, Ava also attended therapy once a week. The type of therapy she received was called CBT (cognitive behavioral therapy). CBT is a highly structured therapy that helps change the way one thinks (cognition) in order to improve one's actions (behavior). During CBT, the therapist

challenges the negative automatic thoughts
and gives practical strategies to modify one's
behavior. Studies show that CBT has the most
evidence for improving one's outcome for
depression, anxiety, and eating disorders.[15]

After a year of treatment, Ava was
a completely different child. At her last
appointment, she was neatly dressed in
appropriate clothing for the weather. She
smiled often while she spoke and made good
eye contact. She told me about her soccer team
and the various clubs she joined at school. Her
parents beamed with pride and told me that
Ava had been eating normal amounts of food
and that she stopped binging and purging.
She naturally lost some weight due to soccer,
and she was within normal weight for her

15 Hofmann, Stefan. "The Efficacy of Cognitive Behavioral Therapy:
A Review of Meta-analyses." *Cognit Ther Res*, vol. 36, no. 5, 2012, pp.
427–440.

age and height. Since they were moving to another state, they came to say goodbye. At the end of the meeting, her father said, "Doc, thank you for all your help. We went through the worst period of our lives before we met you. How I wish there was a book out there that could have prepared me for all this ..."

AFTERWORD
POLICY CHANGES THAT HELP SUPPORT PARENTING

At the frontline of the youth mental health crisis, our children, adolescents, and their families have taken the brunt of the battle thus far. However, they cannot be the only ones holding the fort if we want to make any progress in alleviating this disaster. We also need to get politicians and technology companies involved to assist in this endeavor.

The people who work in technology companies and politicians are likely to have children (or grandchildren) themselves who are struggling. They are in positions to make significant and lasting changes in order to turn the tide. They can create laws to protect and secure children's data and ensure the highest standards for security. Technology companies can develop tools to foster healthy online environments for the youths and make it easier for parents to monitor their children's Internet use.

Parents, friends, and mentors who are supporting a struggling youth can also write to their state representatives to request more transparency from the technology companies to ensure better outcomes.

We've had successful public health campaigns in the past once people felt it was important enough. We have been able to eliminate smallpox since the 1980s. Smallpox was a highly contagious disease that killed hundreds of millions of people over thousands of years. Three out of ten people who had it died. In 1967, WHO launched a plan to eradicate it, and they declared it eliminated in 1980.

Due to collaborative actions around the world, the WHO was able to declare the end of COVID-19 as a global emergency on May 5, 2023. With the concerted effort on all fronts, we have a chance to avert this crisis and possibly see the day when the US Surgeon General announces the end of the mental health crisis in our youth.

WORKS CITED

"2022 National Survey on LGBTQ Youth Mental Health." The Trevor Project, https://www.thetrevorproject.org/survey-2022/. Accessed 18 September 2023.

Boserup, Brad. "Alarming trends in US domestic violence during the COVID-19 pandemic." *The American Journal of Emergency Medicine*, vol. 38, no. 12, 2020, pp. 2753-2755.

Centers for Disease Control and Prevention. "Youth Risk Behavior Surveillance Data Summary & Trends Report: 2009-2019." https://www.cdc.gov/healthyyouth/data/yrbs/pdf/yrbsdatasummarytrendsreport2019-508.pdf.

Curtin, Sally. "State suicide rates among adolescents and young adults aged 10–24: United States, 2000–2018." *National Vital Statistics Reports*, vol. 69, no. 11, p. 3, https://stacks.cdc.gov/view/cdc/93667.

Hensums, Maud. "What Works for Whom in School-Based Anti-bullying Interventions? An Individual Participant Data Meta-analysis." *Prev Sci*, vol. 24, no. 8, 2023, 1435–1446.

Hofmann, Stefan. "The Efficacy of Cognitive Behavioral Therapy: A Review of Meta-analyses." *Cognit Ther Res*, vol. 36, no. 5, 2012, pp. 427–440, https://www.ncbi.nlm.nih.gov/pmc/articles/PMC3584580/.

Ramirez de Arellano, Michael A. "Trauma-Focused Cognitive-Behavioral Therapy for Children and Adolescents: Assessing the

Evidence." *Psychiatric Services*, vol. 65, no. 5, 2014, pp. 591-602, https://doi.org/10.1176/appi.ps.201300255.

Riehm, Kira. "Associations Between Time Spent Using Social Media and Internalizing and Externalizing Problems Among US Youth." *JAMA psychiatry*, vol. 76, no. 12, 2019, 1266-1273., https://jamanetwork.com/journals/jamapsychiatry/fullarticle/2749480.

Roman-Urrestarazu, Andres. "Brain structural deficits and working memory fMRI dysfunction in young adults who were diagnosed with ADHD in adolescence." *European Child & Adolescent Psychiatry*, vol. 25, pp. 529-538, https://doi.org/10.1007/s00787-015-0755-8.

"Social Media and Youth Mental Health: The

US Surgeon General's Advisory." *HHS.gov*, https://www.hhs.gov/sites/default/files/sg-youth-mental-health-social-media-advisory.pdf. Accessed 19 September 2023.

The MTA Cooperative Group. "A 14-month randomized clinical trial of treatment strategies for attention-deficit/hyperactivity disorder. The MTA Cooperative Group. Multimodal Treatment Study of Children with ADHD." *Archives of General Psychiatry*, vol. 56, no. 12, 1999, pp. 1073-86, https://pubmed.ncbi.nlm.nih.gov/10591283/.

"The U.S. Surgeon General's Advisory." *HHS.gov*, 6 December 2021, https://www.hhs.gov/sites/default/files/surgeon-general-youth-mental-health-advisory.pdf. Accessed 19 September 2023.

Trach, J. "Bystander responses to school bullying: A cross-sectional investigation of grade and sex differences." *Canadian Journal of School Psychology*, vol. 25, 2010, pp. 114–130.

Vera, Alonso Zea. "The Phenomenology of Tics and Tic-Like Behavior in TikTok." *Pediatric Neurology*, vol. 130, 2020, pp. 14-20, https://www.pedneur.com/article/S0887-8994(22)00021-2/fulltext.

Yard, Ellen. "Emergency Department Visits for Suspected Suicide Attempts Among Persons Aged 12-25 Years Before and During the COVID-19 Pandemic - United States." *Morbidity and Mortality Weekly Report*, vol. 70, no. 24, 2021, pp. 888-894, https://doi.org/10.15585/mmwr.mm7024e1.

LIST OF RESOURCES

NAMI (National Alliance on Mental Illness) is a national organization that offers mental health resources for adults as well as youths. You can reach the agency by simply searching the Internet for Nami.org or calling 1-800-950-6264.

The mental health crisis number is 988. If one does not want to talk to a counselor on the phone, they can also text 988, and a trained crisis counselor will text them back.
The LiveWell Foundation (tel: 267-530-3739) provides free depression groups for teens, adults, and seniors. These groups are available in person and on Zoom.

If you want to receive only online support, Grieving.com is one of the oldest grief support communities on the Internet.

You can find your state's laws and policies against bullying at the Stopbullying.gov website. The URL for this page is: https://www.stopbullying.gov/resources/laws

Dr. Jean Young Bai is a child and adolescent psychiatrist who works and lives in Pennsylvania. She is on the front lines of the mental health crisis as both a mother of two children and a practitioner. Along with her children, she lives with her husband and a rescued cat.

She has written four children's books under her pen name, Jean Young: *Portals to Wonderland (Books 1,2,3)* and *Squiggy's Challenge*. She had the opportunity to give a talk on her *Portals to Wonderland, Book 2*, at the TRAPPIST-1 astronomy conference in Liege, Belgium, in 2019. *Parenting the Crisis Generation* is her first self-help book.